What Parents, Prin[
Are Saying About T

"The concepts and me[**Life Purpose Discovery books** give youth purpose and direction, which is paramount and of **vital importance for students** in this day and age. It is the missing piece that connects the voids between obtainable information and their life....that **guides them** to know how to turn **information into true knowledge**, which is when one has information and knows what to do with it. The use of the **Doorknob** materials is important for students and teachers with all the changes that are happening in education today by providing guidance, and teaching young people **skills and strategies for a successful life and career**."

> – *Russell Hughes, principal, Walton High School, DeFuniak Springs, Florida*
> *(principal for 10 years in both Middle and High schools, leader of "Grade A" school)*

"I liked your ideas for parenting, and the **clear step-by-step ways** that are presented. Writing them down in an organized way was a very good idea. It seems that it would be easy to stay on track, which means accomplishing the goal, finding and accomplishing one's Life Purpose. In my classroom I had a large picture of a steam engine on a track. Under it the caption read **"Stay on the right track."**

> – *Charlie Beall, parent and retired principal, Prince Georges County Public Schools, Maryland*

"In our fast-paced world, this book is a great reminder to slow down and be a supportive parent who is here to guide our children to know and love who they are... happily I learned a lot about myself in the process!"

> – *Lynn Wisniewski, parent, and owner of Under The Cherry Blossoms bookstore*

10 Easy Keys To Unlocking Kids' Passion & Purpose
www.doorknobbooks.com

i

"This book is a very practical, **straightforward yet profound look into the life of your child** and will assist you in guiding them to becoming fully alive and reaching their potential, seeing themselves as unique, valued and able to have a lasting impact on their world."
> – *Coach Kelly Nevius, parent and President, Home School Sports of California, a physical education program for home-school schools*

"The reason I believe this book will be **helpful to both parents and teachers** alike is that many of our children today have limited social and career skills and now we need to address this problem. It is sad that we have children that are not just failing in one class but several classes because the parents have allowed the children to do as they want. I feel that interaction parent/child and teacher/student needs to be improved.

"Think about it, a four-year college has now turned into a five-six year college and 75% of the students do not even go into the job field that they majored in to get their degree. Many students have changed their majors 2-3 times by the time they graduate college. **All of Teri's books will help us to get a better understanding of our child's Life Purpose and help us to help them succeed.**"
> – *John, parent of one high school and two college students, and business owner*

DOORKNOB®
LIFE PURPOSE BOOKS

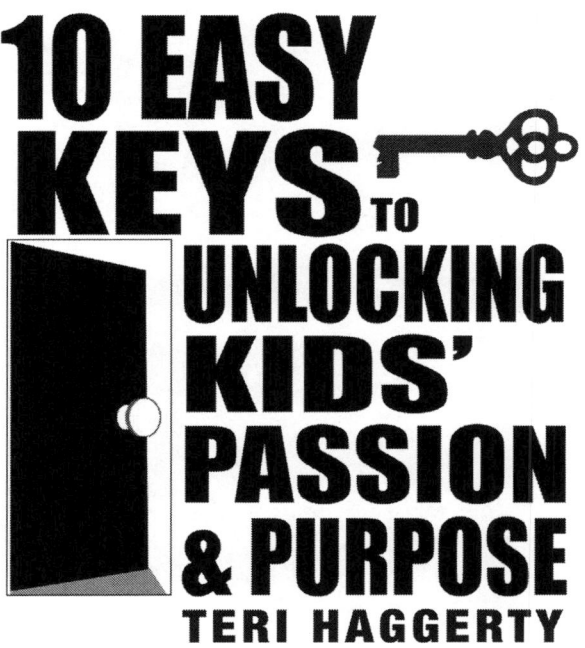

10 EASY KEYS TO UNLOCKING KIDS' PASSION & PURPOSE

TERI HAGGERTY

A Guide for Parents and Teachers

Also by Teri Haggerty:

Your Key, Your Door:
Life Purpose Discovery Book For Teens

and corresponding teaching guides:

• *Instructor's Guide for Parents and Small Groups*
• *Classroom Teacher's Notes for Large Group*
and Classroom Youth Teaching

Life Purpose Discovery Toolkit™ (Audio)

*This book is dedicated to the inspiring students of **Walton High School** of DeFuniak Springs (Florida, U.S.), their principal **Russell Hughes** (shown above— see his comments on page i) and their teachers. Walton High School was the first school to consistently use my first book, **Your Key, Your Door: Life Purpose Discovery Book for Teens**. Over 300 WHS students have used this book to discover how to live a life that will bring passion, fulfillment and purpose throughout their lives.*

Also, to other passionate adults that have inspired me and repeatedly requested an easy parent's and teacher's guide to use to lead their young people to a fulfilling life: Rick W, Sally V, Shalawn B, Sharon C, Laurie M, Bob G, Johnny C, Steven R and my faithful advisory team Ed, Mike, John, Taylor, Honor, Richard, Charlie, Annalee, Trudy and Denny.

DOORKNOB®
LIFE PURPOSE BOOKS

FIRST EDITION
First Printing, 2013
Printed in the United States of America

To order this title *10 Easy Keys To Unlocking Kids'*
Passion & Purpose, please contact:
www.doorknobbooks.com or **www.amazon.com**

Cover Design by Kathy Lyon

ISBN: 978-0-9856235-1-7

How Do You Nurture LIFE in a Child?

Congratulations for taking the initiative to help a child you care about. *It might be your own child, or one that you know* through home, school, church, or elsewhere, *but for the purposes of this book, you are making this child "your child."* Young people in our world today need adults around them who will take the time—with unconditional love—to help them discover their uniqueness and value as they grow. With the right guidance from a caring adult, children can discover that *they hold the key to creating good in their lives and futures* through understanding the personal power of vision and action. By following the guidance in this book, you will truly make a vast difference throughout "your" child's life.

Start by really *"seeing"* your child:

L = LOOK consistently at the experiences your child enjoys, is passionate about or drawn toward. Then...

I = INQUIRE about what those experiences mean to your child and how it makes him or her feel. Next...

F = FOCUS with faith in your child's unique value and help him or her focus on their priorities. Finally...

E = EMPOWER your child by encouraging his or her natural ability to succeed, and helping open doors for him or her.

Once you start to really "see" your child, you'll discover that the *"10 Keys"* in this book really will be easy and fun… and at the same time, a powerful way to unlock your child's passion and purpose.

Acknowledgements

Thanks to the 2012 request by the magazine *Natural Awakenings* for me to write an article on cultivating kid's passion in life (published in Nov. 2012, Pensacola FL) the idea for this second Doorknob book was born.

The need for material on this subject was clear and sought after by adults from many walks of life. My heartfelt appreciation to two beautiful people; my graphic designer Kathy and my editor Trisha for their huge passion to bring this series of life changing books to all ages. Without them these messages and tools would never reach the waiting hands and hearts of the parents and educators of our world.

And again my heartfelt humble thanks goes to that inner voice that speaks and guides me what and how to write the messages needed globally today.

Writer's Advisory Team for Doorknob Books:

Richard T. D'Avanzo, Ph D (Psychology)

Charlie Beall, Ed D (Education)

Honor Bell, US Army Retired, Former Special Assistant
(GS-14) to the Chief of Naval Education

Rev. Dr. Pamela Feeser, Manager, Community Health Ministries in
the Upper Keys, Baptist Health South Florida

Jonathan Gustavson, Technology Advisor

Robert J. Gurski, B.S. Physical Electronics

Trisha Kirby, Editor

Robert Klubenspies, Technology Advisor

Kathy Lyon, Graphic Designer

Arden "Denny" Nelson, Computer Consultant

Kent Nuttall, Curriculum and Programs Manager. MEd. also CPLP

Mike Potters, BA (Psychology) MFT (Family Therapy)

Steven J. Royer, MS Biology

J. Nevin Shaffer, Jr., MBA, Licensed Patent Attorney

Ed Stanford, MS (Counseling and Human Development) MEd
(Educational Leadership)

Table of Contents

Teri Haggerty

HELLO, and **THANK YOU,** parents and teachers, for making the decision to use **10 Easy Keys To Unlocking Kids' Passion & Purpose.**

I welcome you to join me in the magical exploration of helping the children you care about discover and live the life they were born to live.

During the last 30 years, the first ten as a home and public school teacher, and for the last twenty years as a business consultant and certified Life Coach, I have enjoyed many hours working with teens and adults. I have led people of all ages to discover and live the life they want to live and develop the habit of the *"magical life"* of being *themselves*. Some of my other experiences that are the foundation for this book are working as an Organization Development Consultant (MBA, ODL University of West Florida) for Walt Disney World Magic Kingdom, Tulane University, Westinghouse-Hanford, Whirlpool Corporation, and as a Professional Certified Coach (PCC International Coach Federation), Juvenile Justice System in Florida, and many individual youth and adult coaching clients.

I truly believe the ideas in this book will *enhance success* in the *field of education* and *current methods of parenting*. This book will teach new ways

to deepen awareness and skills of supporting, interacting and teaching leadership and responsibility to young people. The result will be a world filled with individuals who are passionate about their life and experience daily and consistent satisfaction, fulfillment and well-being both in their inner-being and interaction with others.

In our business lives, we adults are pretty "bottom-line" focused in our work styles and communication, i.e. "stick to the facts," "be brief," "time is money," etc. But in our **personal lives** and **at school**, that may not serve us so well. In the family and school setting, children need us to take the time to really "see" them and listen to the deep feelings and dreams that they have for their lives. On this foundation and in this space, relationships and young people prosper.

Here and **now** is a perfect place and time to begin your journey to learn more about the wonderful unique person your child is—whether you have one child, several or a whole classroom full! You are right on time with this experience! **Helping them to be the unique person they are is an essential gift that helps a child to breathe a sigh of relief that they have one person who understands them, and a place to relax and be appreciated for who they really are.**

I suggest you read the **Introduction, Conclusion**, and briefly all the **Keys** before you begin this wonderful journey of "seeing" your child. Thank you for caring enough to join me in creating that positive place for all of us to live and thrive.

Teri Haggerty

10 Easy Keys To Unlocking Kids' Passion & Purpose
www.doorknobbooks.com

Introduction:
Being Like Sherlock Holmes

Whether you are a teacher, parent, grandparent, coach, counselor or youth leader you probably have a natural desire to create a lasting impact by helping young people reach their fullest potential. Following clues like the famous Sherlock Holmes detective will help you discover valuable information about your young person that will help them unlock their inner potential.

Young people today can feel stressed and confused as they navigate the many life transitions from childhood to adult. In spite of our best intentions, we sometimes assume we know what our young people are experiencing and are most passionate about, and often we have made incorrect or incomplete conclusions.

As a parent or teacher, one of your most important roles is to lovingly explore with your young person, in a quiet unassuming way, the *essence* of who your child really is. This role of facilitating opportunities and opening doors for them to explore and make discoveries about themselves is a rewarding endeavor.

One of the greatest gifts we can give children and young adults is to help them understand and integrate their life experiences, providing *unconditional love* during this process.

This facilitates their journey to clarify on a daily basis:

1. ***who they are***, and

2. how to best ***express themselves*** in healthy fulfilling ways that fit them.

In this book you will discover powerful techniques and information that will help you be successful in guiding your young person to life success, inner-harmony and wellbeing.

Specifically this book will provide:

🔑 ***Ten easy "Keys"*** that create a natural way to relate to your child on a daily basis. This will enhance their understanding of who they are and encourage them to create, clarify and follow their vision toward their ideal future.

🔑 ***Clear actions*** you can take to create opportunities your child can use to build skills for living with vitality throughout their young years and naturally transitioning successfully into young adulthood.

🔑 ***Non-intrusive ideas*** that will show your commitment to their lives as they instinctively know this is important to their personal development and future success.

🔑 ***"Keys" (Chapters)*** that can be completed in any order that seems best. Some users mark the date they journal in a section for future reference.

Techniques of discovery that are similar to trying to find out what someone wants for their birthday or Christmas without them knowing you are on this quest. If your young person wonders why you are asking your questions, you may explain your intent to understand him or her better because you truly care and love them.

Methods that can be used by adults such as parents, teachers, family members and youth program leaders that are easy and enjoyable as you learn key skills to help your child. The results will lead to years of rewarding experiences as you watch your youngster move into successful adulthood and in turn give back to others in his or her own special ways.

For those that desire a more detailed exploration of these ideas with weekly step-by-step exercises for youth, please use the book ***Your Key, Your Door, Life Purpose Discovery Book for Teens*** by Teri Haggerty at *www.doorknobbooks.com* or *www.amazon.com*. This engaging 20-chapter workbook will give you and your young person specific ***exercises for the young person to do*** to understand their unique Life Purpose and how to apply this purpose in decision making and life planning. Each chapter takes about an hour. A detailed instructor's guide is also available as a free download from the doorknob books web site. User testimonials describe the book as fun, easy-to-use, powerful and rewarding. This book is ideal for youth ages 8-21.

Current Research

The recent Gallup Student Poll, published in 2012, cites their ten-year study showing three critical factors for student success: **hope, engagement** and **well-being**. *Hope* was attributed to be a more robust predictor of college success than high school GPA, SAT and ACT scores. *Engagement* and *well-being* scores predict their probable success in high school and beyond. Only one third of all students tested by Gallup currently have these three combined factors.

By using this book, you can help your child increase these three important factors—**hope, engagement** and **well-being**—on a daily basis, which may also benefit their scholastic experience as a natural outcome.

Key Facts: Essential Concepts for Success with this Book

1. Young people have an important need that may be far above those we normally assume are top priority. This critical need is to be deeply **_"seen"_** by significant others around them. This "seeing" is simple to do.

2. "Seeing" is done in moments of time when you **_pause, with unconditional love, to be deeply present and aware_** of your child in whatever they are feeling or doing. Take an opportunity to ask and notice what an experience means to your child. Don't be surprised when often it may have a different meaning to them than what it may appear to you. Their answer is always right in their mind, no matter how much you may not understand.

3. Using this book it will be easy to **_record, organize_** and **_reflect_** on the **_discoveries_** you make about your child. **_This is your work not theirs._** Using these **_10 Keys_** you will learn to **_"lovingly see"_** your child by asking what an experience means **_to them_**. This will become a healthy habit as you practice. Each **_"Key"_** provides powerful questions that will help you and your child to see, clarify and cherish their unique talents, personality traits and emotions. Take moments along the way to show love by celebrating their uniqueness.

_4._ Instead of viewing your child's experiences in terms of success or failure, you and your child can **_choose to value all their experiences_** as perfect

opportunities to examine and make on-going choices that best fit who they are. Release the tendency to judge your child or their experiences. In this loving, supporting space, give them room to **explore** and **gain wisdom** from the outcomes of their varied choices each day. In this way they will learn the skills that bring them joy and balance in life, walk with courage and focus, and find their own ways to give back to others. Remember, your child **cannot "fail"** because they are **learning**, and learning is what success is all about. Success is simply the joy of life's journey regardless of what "appears" to be a success or failure.

5. Even the "toughest" child will respond in time to these inspirational techniques as a way to explore their unique value to themselves, the earth and humanity.

6. Remember each child is here for a reason often unclear to us when they are young. The daily gift we can give them is to lovingly guide them on a path of learning self-leadership, how to live a purposeful life of **being who they are,** faithfulness to their **unique** qualities and values, and discovering ways of giving back to others.

7. Remember that a life is only limited by thinking and beliefs. Children are not usually as hindered by these limiting thoughts until they get older. You may help your child by modeling a **positive** and **abundance mindset** that enhances the child's growth. When you notice fear-based thoughts arising in your mind, choose instead to speak encouraging words to your child. You may not know how their vision will work out, but

give it time, a little faith, encouragement, and watch as their journey unfolds. Some dreams take time to materialize and it is a person's sustained belief in their dreams and goals that brings them into reality.

8. There are many books that guide parents and teachers in their role and responsibilities for the health and care of children. This book will not review those teachings, but rather *goes much deeper* to the critical aspect of *caring for the heart and soul* of young people so they learn to have a sustainable sense of *well-being,* growing up as powerful thinkers and courageous decision-makers, who are *engaged* in healthful ways with school and life.

9. Your child will learn to own *personal responsiblity* for their choices, healthy attitudes and well-being.

10. These personal responsibilities will help your child learn to live a life of hope, passion and purpose. *Creating awareness of their gifts* and how to use them puts them on a path to a life of health and happiness.

11. Once aware of their gifts, your child can begin to discover their future career path, leading to improved *engagement in school* and *enhanced scholastic success.* Thus, the *motivation for success comes from within* them as they see how their classwork specifically fits into their future life path.

12. The *10 Keys* will give you guidance to asking *powerful questions* in ways that are safe and valuable, making your job of parenting or teaching much easier and more joyful.

13. *Bottom-line desired result for parents:* To learn the practice of continually and lovingly *seeing* your child and helping them naturally clarify who they are and how to live a life that fits their unique *essence* of being.

14. *Bottom-line desired result for teachers and others:* Student engagement with your teaching will increase as they understand why your subject is important to their journey toward their ideal life and career. Behavior problems often subside as the student becomes more focused on your curriculum or program.

Book Design and Ultimate Purpose:
A "Take With You" Parent/Teacher Companion

This powerful little book was deliberately designed to be *small, easy to carry and available*, so you can *IMMEDIATELY JOURNAL* the words and essence of your child's experience so they are not forgotten. It's amazing how you think you'll remember a few words your child said, only to find that later the *exact* words and meaning have slipped away. The exact words are important and give the best clues to specifics of your child's inner thoughts, and true insights into who they are.

When working with a client in my coaching practice, I am always *ready to write when a client says something*, for I've discovered that often the heart speaks *once*, and when I ask them to repeat, they can't remember exactly what they just said. Profound wording and depth can easily be lost. As you become a "coach" to your child by using this book, practice developing this invaluable habit of preparedness, deep listening skills and journaling!

Key 1: Discovering Your Child's Dream Life List

- Over time, consistently take a few minutes when you and your child are together to **ask your child what are some things they envision doing, experiencing or how they would like to help someone/something in their lifetime.** This is like the **"bucket list"** you may have heard about.

- Make this a natural conversation, possibly when you are traveling or during a relaxed time together. This may happen over several days, weeks or months to get an abundance of ideas. Invite them to tell you later as they think of more!

- Remember to never criticize their ideas. Lovingly watch their hearts open like flowers to the sun with your questions! Your unconditional love, genuine curiosity and focused "seeing" are like rays of sunlight warming their souls.

- **As quickly as possible, record** what your child shares with you on the lines on the next page. This is not an assignment for them to do, but rather a place for **you to record** so you remember what they said. (If you desire exercises that your young person will do themselves, consider exploring the **_Your Key, Your Door_** book, mentioned in the introduction). This will give you a few beginning clues to your child's path of life choices. Keep these ideas **confidential** between you and your child unless they give you permission to share with others. If, for some reason, you don't have this book with you at the time of your conversation, write it on a scrap of paper and re-write into this journal as soon as you can.

Journal: **Your Child's Dream Life List and Date of Entry**

1. _____

2. _____

3. _____

4. _____

5. _____

6. _____

7. _____

8. _____

9. _____

10. _____

11. _____

12. _____

Journal: Your Child's Dream Life List and Date of Entry *(continued)*

13. _____

14. _____

15. _____

16. _____

17. _____

18. _____

19. _____

20. _____

21. _____

22. _____

23. _____

24. _____

25. _____

26. _____

27. _____

Now, let your child be an example for you to broaden your horizons! Even though you are an adult you too can reach for your heart's desires! Kids see no limits until they learn them from adults. Follow their example!

List a few things ***you*** would like to do, experience or help accomplish in the next few years of your life!

Journal: **Parent/Teacher Dream Life List**

1. _____

2. _____

3. _____

4. _____

5. _____

6. _____

7. _____

8. _____

9. _____

10. _____

11. _____

12. _____

Make it visual, for real inspiration!

If desired, you can help your child to use a large piece of poster paper and cut and glue pictures from magazines of places and experiences they would like to have in their lifetime. This activity can be done over a length of time. Be interested in their picture choices, and avoid judging, criticizing or discouraging their selections.

Post this board where your child can see it everyday. A vision board like this begins the attraction process of these things and can inspire your child to begin moving toward these experiences with inspired planning and actions. Let this happen naturally! Help them expect good things—like the pictures they've chosen—and more good things and experiences will come to them. *Life is good if you expect it to be!*

Notes:

Key 2: Exploring Life Purpose Awareness– The Key to Success

When your child is doing something that they love to do or having an experience that is wonderful for them, this reveals something about who they are. To be more clear on this and pin down specific details, take a few moments and ask your child how they **felt** and **why** that experience was important to them. Help your child be aware of times when they are doing things that they are passionate about. Ask them:

1. How they **felt** in that experience, and

2. **Why** this experience was important to them— what value did **they** receive from it?

Their answers give clues to the basic core **"essence"** of who they are and their **"Life Purpose" is to live it**!

It's also important for your child to learn how to make mandatory life experiences, such as going to school and doing home chores, fit who they are (sometimes we have things we have to do and yet often we have flexibility in how it gets done). Just like plants need to be in the right location to thrive, children and young adults thrive with the right experiences done in the best way for them.

For their benefit, watch for times they are enjoying an experience and times when they are happy while

reaching out to help others. A variety of experiences that they enjoy and which reflect these core attributes of their "essence" can lead them to develop a habit of wise decision-making. This valuable habit cultivates a life of success and healthy inner well-being.

Using this technique, adults can ask these powerful questions which open the child's awareness of choices they are making that fulfill **who they are,** both in their personal life and as they begin to explore ideas of future careers.

An example: Several young people on a team described that their passion is to play basketball. But they gave the following different answers as to **WHY** *it was important to them—the #2 question:*

- *One boy said that his basketball experience was special because he could* **accomplish something with his teammates** *(revealing a possible team-oriented personality).*

- *Another child said it was because she could get* **instant feedback** *on her skill of hitting the basket (indicating a person who likes prompt feedback on performance).*

- *The third young person said he liked the feeling of challenging and* **exercising his body** *(possibly revealing a physically active person).*

They were all passionate about playing basketball but for **different reasons** *—each youth had a different*

*core reason they like to play. They like playing basketball because it puts them in a place that "fits" their personality and their **essence**.*

In their lives your child will discover the experiences they are passionate about that will reflect their unique core "essence." Over time, your young person will develop the skill of making choices based on what they have learned about who they are. For example, the young basketball player who liked working with the team might choose working in a different team setting to again enjoy accomplishing something important— because working with a team fits **who he is**.

When journaling your child's experiences and their reasons why those experiences are important, be sure to note their words and phrases as **positives**. For example: *"I didn't mess up and hurt my team"* (a negative phrase) can be easily flipped to *"I learned a new skill"* (a positive phrase). Often a person's mind will first express an idea as a negative, but then can easily reword it to a positive phrase.

Career and activities we all experience in life are enjoyable because they allow us to naturally express who we are at the deepest level. The more an experience fits who we are, the better it feels deep within our hearts during and after we do it.

The following pages will help you as you begin observing and journaling the **WHAT** and the **WHY** of several of your child's experiences. Notice two types of experiences:

1. Activities focused on the young person that they enjoy and are doing for **themselves**, and

2. Activities that they enjoy where they are helping **others**.

All people, even young people, need to receive the positive feeling from choosing to do activities and have experiences that fit who they are. Then, from that positive, happy and fullfilled place, they can give out to others in a way that naturally fits them. This is a healthy, balanced way to live life—in the flow of positive Life Purpose energy.

Journal:
Noticing Your Child's Experiences

When you notice over the next few weeks and months when your child is having a ***good experience***, ask the reason and record their answers here. (There is a list of "feeling words" on page 122 in the ***Appendix*** that can help you and your child articulate a feeling.) If desired, you can ask about significant previous experiences as well. Here's an example:

Example Experience:
Simple description: *Basketball practice*

Date: *Friday 10/19/13*

How did your child say they ***felt*** in that experience?
appreciated (good team player)
healthy, excited (big game on Sat.)

Why was that experience ***important*** to them?

What ***value*** was received?: *gained skills,*
connected with his friends
and helped his team

Experience #1:

Simple description: _____

_____

Date: _____

How did your child say they *felt* in that experience?

_____

_____

_____

_____

Why was that experience *important* to them?

What *value* was received?: _____

_____

_____

_____

_____

_____

_____

Experience #2:

Simple description: _____

_____

Date: _____

How did your child say they *felt* in that experience?

_____

_____

_____

_____

Why was that experience *important* to them?

What *value* was received?: _____

_____

_____

_____

_____

_____

_____

Experience #3:

Simple description: _____ _____

_____

Date: _____

How did your child say they *felt* in that experience?

_____

_____

_____

_____

Why was that experience *important* to them?

What *value* was received?: _____

_____

_____

_____

_____

_____

_____

Experience #4:

Simple description: _____

_____

Date: _____

How did your child say they *felt* in that experience?

_____

_____

_____

_____

Why was that experience *important* to them?

What *value* was received?: _____

_____

_____

_____

_____

_____

_____

Experience #5:

Simple description: _____

_____

Date: _____

How did your child say they *felt* in that experience?

_____

_____

_____

_____

Why was that experience *important* to them?

What *value* was received?: _____

_____

_____

_____

_____

_____

_____

Experience #6:

Simple description: _____

_____

Date: _____

How did your child say they *felt* in that experience?

_____

_____

_____

_____

Why was that experience *important* to them?

What *value* was received?: _____

_____

_____

_____

_____

_____

How to Use What You Journaled in Key 2:

The feelings and explanations of why an experience was important to them are the actual words that describe the **essence** of your child's core personhood. **This is who they are.** Like the elements of earth listed on the Periodic Table, each young person is unique in their essence.

It's important to also understand that **the specific words** that your child has shared with you and that you have captured in your journaling **are the words that describe their unique life path**.

The more experiences they have as they grow that **reflect these specific elements of who they are** (described in the words they shared with you), the better their life will be, and the easier your parenting or teaching role will be. Over time you will begin to notice that some of these words or phrases describe them better than others they have shared. Use these specific words to guide them in making daily life choices.

In the basketball practice example, the parent might help this child make a future decision by discussing whether that choice has aspects of the specific words the child shared: "feeling appreciated, healthy, excited, gaining skills, connecting or helping his team." If yes, it is a decision that fits that child and will probably be satisfying for him or her.

Use the words you journaled when listening to your child in Experiences 1-6 as criteria to help them make the best choices along their future path.

More details about the process of writing a full
Life Purpose Statement that may be used as a
guide to future plans and life choices can be found
in the ***Your Key, Your Door*** book mentioned in the
Introduction.

My Perfect Day

Another fun way to explore your child's heart
is to ask them to share with you a description of
"My Perfect Day." This is a description of a day
as they would want it if they could ***make that day
anything they could imagine.*** This is a day where
they can choose to live it in ***any way they desire***
and ***there is no scarcity***—thus lack of money or
time is not a barrier to the story.

Example ideas: Where would they spend the day,
with whom, doing what? What would they be
wearing, eating, traveling in, hearing, sensing,
touching? Basically the sky's the limit! This will
remind them of things they love to do and
experiences they may have had that they enjoyed.

Journal your child's words and ideas: _____

_____

_____

_____

_____

_____

_____

_____

_____

_____

What patterns do you see in your child's story?
(food, travel, friends, animals, nature, etc.)

_____

_____

_____

_____

_____

_____

See examples of "My Perfect Day" as described by
several ninth-grade children on pages 123-125 in
the *Appendix*.

Notes:

Notes:

Key 3: Using Spare Time –A Valuable Asset for Learning Life and Career Skills

Your child's **spare time** is a valuable asset to helping them learn critical skills which may be important aspects of their future career. Research shows that the average child is either watching TV or on the computer for up to **seven hours a day.** Spending hours playing computer games or watching TV may be wasting these valuable learning hours.

Encourage your child to spend their spare time exploring hobbies and doing activities that they feel passionate about. These new activities will naturally replace others that may be robbing them of critical skill-building for their future careers.

Let your child explore a variety of hobbies over time to help them discover and build important skills. They may choose things you may not relate to, but give it a try and remember to explore **why** this hobby or activity interests them! Trust your child's intuition that even an "unusual" activity will help them learn an important aspect of themselves or bring a new skill into focus.

Your young person may like crafts, sewing with a neighbor or grandparent, building things with building materials or construction type toys, microscopes, insect collecting, surfing, outdoor activities, traditional sports, horseback riding, musical instruments, writing, art, drawing, drama, youth clubs, and the list goes on and on. (See *Activity/Hobby list* on pages 126-127 in the ***Appendix*).

Spare time hours are defined as those after school, homework and household chores. There may be several of these hours every day and more on weekends—on average, this adds up to over 1,000 hours in a year's time! Ask your child in a friendly conversation to tell you some activities or hobbies they'd like to try over the next few months or year. Journal the ideas they give you. Then help them pick an activity or hobby to **start doing now** in their spare time after school, on weekends and in the summer months. Celebrate with love their learning and share time with them doing some of the activity. Help them notice how their natural skills increase and their natural tendencies toward this activitiey might turn into a career one day.

Example: A successful career Navy seaman started designing with building sets when he was four years old. By age twelve, he was building experimental kit radios which he continued through his high school years. He received his amateur radio novice license by age sixteen. After high school he joined the Navy, and was very thankful for the skills, wisdom and knowledge he had learned by the time he was eighteen. These skills became the foundation of a successful career, and were learned in his spare time activities as a child and through his association with supportive adults.

Your child or young adult may mention ideas that are costly. Refrain from saying it is "too expensive," but rather start with some aspect that is convenient for your budget. Ask a friend or relative that is familiar with that activity to allow your child to participate with them. There is always research that can be done at the library, community service organizations and local youth agencies that may assist you with moving forward with a specific interest. Trust your child's interest and intuition. ***Where there is a will there is always a way!***

Journal: Noticing Your Child's Interests

List here the interests and hobbies your child mentions they would like to try. Then prioritize the list below:

#_____ _____

#_____ _____

#_____ _____

#_____ _____

#_____ _____

#_____ _____

#_____ _____

Allow the child to choose one of these interests or hobbies to start with or follow the directions on the Activity/Hobby List from pages 126 and 127 in the ***Appendix***, and write the chosen activity here:

_____

Discuss with your child how they would like to start their chosen interest, and list the first action step to get this hobby started on the next page.

Next, discuss with your child a consistent time they would like to spend with this activity, during their spare time (after school, weekends, summer vacation, etc). As you manage your classroom (if you are a teacher) or family's schedule, be sure to allow for this important learning time. It may be helpful to create and post a time chart on the wall to show a week's routine that includes time for this spare time hobby, school homework, and other important activities.

There may be things that are currently scheduled in your child's life that you may want to discontinue and replace with a better use of time for hobbies and these chosen activities. If in time their interest wanes, go back to their hobby/activity list, and encourage them to try

Chosen Interest or Hobby:

_____

Possible Action Steps to Begin:

1. _____

2. _____

3. _____

4. _____

5. _____

6. _____

Ask your child to choose one of the steps above.

Chosen Action Step:

_____

Best Consistent Scheduled Time:
(See example Weekly Planning Chart on pages
128-129 in the *Appendix*.)

_____

   Encourage them to take action on this first
step! In time, you may want to begin to explore and
discuss a career that this hobby or passion might
lead to. You will be doing this as a more in-depth
exercise in *Key 4*.

something new. Encourage them to try this activity/ hobby for a length of time if their interest continues.

As you examine how your child best spends his or her daily hours, ***please read "Spare Key #2"*** at the end of this book about the importance for young people to spend time directly interacting with nature, and including this critical activity in their weekly schedule.

Notes:

Key 4:
Celebrating Natural and
Learned Skills

Notice over time the skills your child is naturally developing and demonstrating in their daily life and the activities from **Key #3**. This is an aspect of the "seeing" and celebrating their uniqueness. Allow them to use their skills and celebrate success in their daily family life or school experiences.

Celebrating a child's natural skills and talents encourages them to value themselves and see how they contribute to the world.

The skills a young person is interested in learning and develops during youth are often an ideal foundation for their future careers.

Journal: Your Child's Natural Abilities and Skills

Describe some natural ***abilities*** and learned ***skills*** you see in your child or young adult. Add what you observe to this list over time.

1. _____

2. _____

3. _____

4. _____

5. _____

6. _____

7. _____

8. _____

9. _____

10. _____

11. _____

12. _____

13. _____

14. _____

15. _____

16. _____

17. _____

18. _____

19. _____

20. _____

21. _____

22. _____

23. _____

24. _____

25. _____

26. _____

27. _____

28. _____

29. _____

30. _____

31. _____

Over time, list ways that you think you can help your child naturally notice, use and celebrate these skills and how they are helpful in your family or classroom system. This may increase self-esteem and positive behaviors!

1. _____

2. _____

3. _____

4. _____

5. _____

6. _____

7. _____

8. _____

9. _____

10. _____

11. _____

12. _____

13. _____

14. _____

List several ways these skills may apply to their school work, future career or life path. Share your observations with your child on an on-going basis.

1. _____

2. _____

3. _____

4. _____

5. _____

6. _____

7. _____

8. _____

9. _____

10. _____

　　　Words of encouragement are very important to children and young people. List words you can say to let your child know you love and care about them, using their skills and natural talents as your subject. Watch their "cup of love" overflow with this type of "seeing" and appreciation! *Take time to communicate in this way every day.*

Noticing Career Skills

Have a light-hearted discussion with your child about careers that interest them and that they would like to know more about.

#1 Career:_____

1. What are some skills that a person in that career might have learned *in their spare time* activities or hobbies *during their childhood or youth* that is now helping them be successful? If possible, ask someone in this career this question.

_____

_____

_____

_____

_____

2. What are the skills a person in this career would need that would likely be learned *as an adult?*

_____

_____

_____

_____

#2 Career:_____

1. What are some skills that a person in that career might have *learned in their spare time* activities or hobbies *during their childhood or youth* that is now helping them be successful? If possible, ask someone in this career this question.

_____

_____

_____

_____

_____

2. What are the skills a person in this career would need that would be learned *as an adult?*

_____

_____

_____

_____

_____

_____

#3 Career:_____

1. What are some skills that a person in that career might have *learned in their spare time* activities or hobbies *during their childhood or youth* that is now helping them be successful? If possible, ask someone in this career this question.

_____

_____

_____

_____

_____

2. What are the skills a person in this career would need that would be learned *as an adult?*

_____

_____

_____

_____

_____

_____

_____

#4 Career:_____

1. What are some skills that a person in that career might have *learned in their spare time* activities or hobbies *during their childhood or youth* that is now helping them be successful? If possible, ask someone in this career this question.

_____

_____

_____

_____

_____

2. What are the skills a person in this career would need that would be learned *as an adult?*

_____

_____

_____

_____

_____

_____

#5 Career:_____

1. What are some skills that a person in that career might have *learned in their spare time* activities or hobbies *during their childhood or youth* that is now helping them be successful? If possible, ask someone in this career this question.

_____

_____

_____

_____

_____

2. What are the skills a person in this career would need that would be learned *as an adult?*

_____

_____

_____

_____

_____

_____

#6 Career:_____

1. What are some skills that a person in that career might have *learned in their spare time* activities or hobbies *during their childhood or youth* that is now helping them be successful? If possible, ask someone in this career this question. Ask someone in this career this question if possible.

_____

_____

_____

_____

2. What are the skills a person in this career would need that would be learned *as an adult?*

_____

_____

_____

_____

Circle the skills in Exercises 1-6 that your young person seems to like or be interested in developing!

Learning The Skills Your Child Will Find Helpful In Their Future Career

What skills did your child or young person observe and say that they might be interested in learning for their future career? What hobbies or activities would be helpful in learning those skills? How can their spare time (after school, weekends, semester break, summer vacation) be used to develop these skills? This may give you additional ideas to select activities in *Key 3*.

1. Skill: _____

_____

Activity/Hobby: _____

_____

_____

_____

_____

_____

_____

2. Skill: _____

_____

Activity/Hobby: _____

_____

_____

_____

_____

_____

3. Skill: _____

Activity/Hobby: _____

_____

_____

_____

_____

_____

Use this information as appropriate to help open opportunities as your child makes decisions about how to use their spare time in *Key 3*.

Notes:

Key 5:
Seeing Into Your Child's
Future Career Path

Starting at a young age—even as early as age seven or eight—begin encouraging your child to observe the many working people around them. This could include professions such as doctors, dentists, artists, musicians, clerks, repair techs, teachers, athletes, farmers and more. Take time to expose them to working people that may be out of their usual "orbit." Encourage your child to develop their observation skills, which will be a foundation for later job explorations.

For older children, you might arrange a "job shadow" experience, in which they actually meet and talk with professionals in careers and jobs that interest them. This can be done by phone or in person.

Then, go a little deeper! Ask them what they ***liked*** and ***did not like*** about aspects of what they observed about each job or career, and make notes on the journal pages that follow. Encourage and help them do as many of these job shadows as possible over time—ten to twenty is a good beginning! Your friends and neighbors may have very interesting careers to tell about!

Helping your young person to develop this ***observation*** technique can provide important clues about what their future career path might look like, and creates habits of awareness.

Journal: Job Shadow Observations

Record your observations of your child's reaction to these "job shadows:"

#1 Job Shadow:
What aspects about this career does your child *LIKE*?

1. _____

2. _____

3. _____

4. _____

5. _____

6. _____

7. _____

What aspects about these careers does your child *NOT LIKE*?

1. _____

2. _____

3. _____

4. _____

5. _____

#2 Job Shadow:
What aspects about this career does your
child *LIKE*?

1. _____

2. _____

3. _____

4. _____

5. _____

6. _____

7. _____

8. _____

What aspects about these careers does
your child *NOT LIKE*?

1. _____

2. _____

3. _____

4. _____

5. _____

#3 Job Shadow:
What aspects about this career does your child *LIKE*?

1. _____
2. _____
3. _____
4. _____
5. _____
6. _____
7. _____
8. _____

What aspects about these careers does your child *NOT LIKE*?

1. _____
2. _____
3. _____
4. _____
5. _____
6. _____

#4 Job Shadow:
What aspects about this career does your
child **_LIKE_**?

1. _____

2. _____

3. _____

4. _____

5. _____

6. _____

7. _____

8. _____

What aspects about these careers does
your child **_NOT LIKE_**?

1. _____

2. _____

3. _____

4. _____

5. _____

#5 Job Shadow:

What aspects about this career does your child *LIKE*?

1. _____

2. _____

3. _____

4. _____

5. _____

6. _____

7. _____

8. _____

What aspects about these careers does your child *NOT LIKE*?

1. _____

2. _____

3. _____

4. _____

5. _____

6. _____

If your child does a "job shadow" experience, encourage them to write a positive and appreciative *thank you note* (see instructions on pages 130-131 in the *Appendix*) to the person they shadowed (and the person who facilitated the job shadow experience, if there was one), expressing gratitude for their time and sharing as appropriate. This is *best done within three days* of the job shadow experience.

Notes:

10 Easy Keys To Unlocking Kids' Passion & Purpose ⚷

Key 6:
Seeing The Life/School/
Career Connection

One valuable outcome of these "job shadow" experiences happens when a young person realizes that there may be several wonderful careers that will bring them great satisfaction.

When young people observe real life careers, and the skills and training that adults have acquired to support their work, they understand the importance of their various school classes and **how the school work they do today applies to their future**.

This awareness increases engagement with classes and brings hope and excitement for their future. Even when some coursework may be challenging, academic performance is easier when a student is engaged with their studies. This is a success factor mentioned in the Gallup poll referred to earlier, in the **Introduction**.

Example: Recently, a student was struggling with math in fifth grade. When he did some research into the NASA (U.S. space program) student intern program resulting from his Dream Life List conversation with his mom in **Key 1***, he understood the importance of math in this career area that interested him. His increased enthusiasm and change of attitude for math resulted in an easier time with homework and an improvement in his math class grades.*

Over time you can easily and naturally help your child **understand the connection between their current studies and their future career dreams and goals**. Ask your child how they see their studies

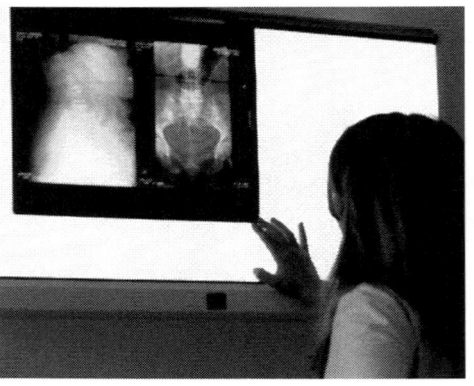

supporting their future career and life path. Encourage them through the hard classes with the vision of how aspects of that class may help them find satisfaction in their life. "Connecting the dots" in your child's mind is a real boost to their scholastic efforts and tenacity.

Journal: **Making the Connections Between School and Future Career**

List the connections your child understands below so you will remember and can use these ideas later as challenging subjects appear in their class schedule:

1. _____
2. _____
3. _____
4. _____
5. _____
6. _____
7. _____
8. _____
9. _____
10. _____

Notice and celebrate when you see your child striving through a subject—whether easy or tough —as they begin to understand how this skill or information will be helpful in their future.

Notes:

Key 7:
Developing The Habits of
Tenacity and Perseverance

We have such a "fast food—instant gratification" society that **tenacity** and **perseverance** are skills that often need strengthening. Encourage your child to take on a project **of their choice** that takes some time—a few weeks or more. Not getting something finished instantly and working consistently over time teaches persistence, tenacity and how to learn from "failure" and move forward. These are important qualities for their future.

Encourage them along the way and celebrate their small successes and "failures." Remember "failure" is part of succeeding and there is no "failure" as long as there is learning taking place.

Examples of projects might include building a model, writing a small book, repairing a broken simple appliance, sewing, training a pet, latchhooking, painting, refinishing an old piece of furniture, etc.

Journal: Self-Enhancement Project Ideas

What are some projects your child has mentioned an interest in that might allow them to build the skills of persistence and tenacity? List these below as you have ongoing conversations together, then have your child select the one they'd like to begin with, and when they would like to start. Encourage them to spend time ***consistently*** on this project, possibly working together with you some of the time until the project is finished. Select another when the first project is finished, and so on:

1. _____

2. _____

3. _____

4. _____

5. _____

6. _____

7. _____

8. _____

9. _____

What ***positive*** qualities did you see in your child that you can celebrate with them that helped them stay persistent, solve problems, and kept them from giving up on their project over time? Share with your child what you've observed to encourage them.

1. _____

2. _____

3. _____

4. _____

5. _____

6. _____

7. _____

8. _____

9. _____

10. _____

11. _____

12. _____

Notes:

Key 8:
Noticing How Your Child
Makes A Difference

8

Your child needs to know their life already makes a difference in the world. It's important for you to help them be aware that they are truly making a positive impact. First, take time to notice how your child makes a difference in this world. Second, let them know **specifically** what difference you observe they are making and its' impact on yourself and others.

Examples might include: emptying the dishwasher, sweeping the floor, helping with house cleaning, caring for pets, talking to grandparents, opening a door for others, sharing, helping siblings, running errands at home or school, keeping their promises, being honest, saying please and thank you, etc.

Noticing and encouraging positive behaviors is much more beneficial in affecting change than criticizing negative ones. Use the journaling space on the next pages to list ways you have noticed how your child makes a positive difference in your life. Express what you see frequently, with a word of appreciation, a hug, a high five, by doing something to help them, or with a small gift—not as a "reward," but as a "just because" surprise! Again, by your doing this, their "love cup" stays full.

Journal: How Your Child Makes A Difference

List some positive differences that you notice your child makes in your life and the world around them. It may be helpful to include the date you list this information, so you can recognize patterns over time.

1. _____

2. _____

3. _____

4. _____

5. _____

6. _____

7. _____

8. _____

9. _____

10. _____

11. _____

12. _____

13 _____

14. _____

15. _____

16. _____

17. _____

18. _____

19. _____

20. _____

21. _____

22. _____

23. _____

Make sure you tell them specifically and consistently how you notice and *appreciate them*. Also, help them notice and appreciate *how others are making a difference in their lives*, and *encourage them to express their appreciation.* It doesn't matter how small or large the contribution may be. Ask them ways that they are contributing that you may not be noticing or aware of!

Notes:

Key 9:

Building Communication Skills
—Genuine Listening

Creating opportunities to truly dialogue with your child about something they believe is one of the deepest and most meaningful ways to connect with them.

Conversations will be easier when you consider that there are four basic communication skills:

1. Reading   3. Speaking
2. Writing   4. Listening

As mentioned in other **Keys**, being **"seen"** with unconditional love by another person using deep listening skills is critical to a child's development and well-being. Practicing their own listening skills is also important for their future success.

Listening is often the weakest communication skill in our society! Research shows that the increased time on computers and with technology is creating a lack of listening skills in today's youth. This **Key** will help you and your child develop these important communication tools.

Daily, weekly or several times a month, take about ten minutes to deeply listen to your child about whatever they want to talk about. Don't judge or criticize the ideas they share. Just listen with a quiet mind and when they finish, reflect back to them what you think they are expressing and feeling through their words, body language, tone and emotions. **No problem-solving is needed here** unless they ask for your help. Remember to take time to listen **without judgement** to their sharing of what's important in their day.

   Swap roles and let them listen to you for five minutes with the same technique. This will cultivate a skill that will help them build success in relationships and their career, while learning from others' experiences. They will be thankful they learned this valuable skill of listening at a young age!

   Sample topics for your child: school experiences, hobbies, someone interesting they have met or would like to meet, an idea that has recently come into their

mind, a worry they have, current events, a friendship they enjoy or a recent activity.

   Celebrate and notice their skill and growth over time and practice in this important area.

Journal: Ideas to Remember from These Listening Experiences

List specific observations about your child's chosen topics, and what you have learned.

1. _____

2. _____

3. _____

4. _____

5. _____

6. _____

7. _____

8. _____

9. _____

10. _____

11. _____

12. _____

13. _____

14. _____

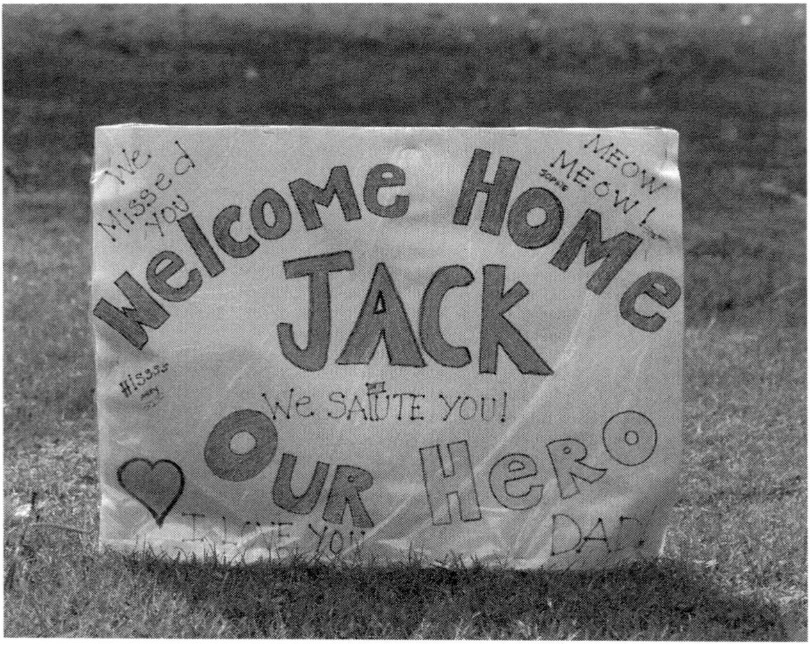
We Missed YOU
MEOW MEOW
Welcome Home
JACK
We SALUTE YOU!
OUR HERO

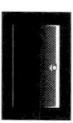

Notes:

Key 10:
Using The Hero Connection

Have a conversation with your child about their heroes and what they admire about them. Their heroes may be from history, sacred writings, television, super heroes and heroines, and real people they may actually know. This conversation will give you clues into **what** traits attract your child's attention and **why**.

What about this "hero" is important, **what aspect** do they admire about them, and **why** is this important?

Help them see where their hero may have qualities and traits that were developed over time, with persistence and passion. Your child may already have some of these qualities that they admire in themselves, that simply need to be identified and nurtured. By using these qualities to guide their decisions and life choices, they will actually be learning from their heroes and enhancing their own character.

Reading stories together of current or historical heroes is a great way to start a conversation. Discuss the heroes they are interested in. Resist criticizing their choices and focus on each hero's **_positive aspects._** (Nobody is perfect, not even heroes!) Your child's perspective may be different from yours. In time, because of your love, support and connecting, any heroes that you identify as a bit negative will fall away. Be patient, have courage, and have faith in the good-

ness and wisdom of your child! Your faith in them will encourage them to recognize these beautiful qualities in themselves, and help bring them to the surface.

Journal: Positive Traits Learned from Their "Heroes" to Apply In Their Lives

Who are your child's heroes? What traits does your child admire? What positive traits would they like to apply in their lives that will help them on their life path? These may not be traits that necessarily resonate as top priorities with you; ***honor your child's unique perspective.***

1. _____

2. _____

3. _____

4. _____

5. _____

6. _____

7. _____

8. _____

9. _____

10. _____

11. _____

What traits of their heroes do they **not** want to copy in their lives? (No hero is perfect!)

1. _____

2. _____

3. _____

4. _____

5. _____

6. _____

What character qualities does your child think would be important for them to copy in their lives as they think about their *future career* or *life choices*? These may be some demonstrated by their heroes or ones they think of on their own.

1. _____

2. _____

3. _____

4. _____

5. _____

6. _____

7. _____

8. _____

9. _____

10. _____

11. _____

12. _____

13. _____

In addition to the **Key** concepts found in this book there are a several other sources of great material to be familiar with when parenting or teaching young people. The next two **Spare Keys** will describe these books and ideas briefly so that you may be aware of their availability to assist your efforts to bring love and support to your child, and how they may be used while doing this **_10 Easy Keys_** book.

Spare Key 1:
Your Child's "Love Languages"

Five Different Ways To Show Love

The theme of this book is that what your child or young person needs more than anything else along with being "seen" is to be *loved unconditionally by at least one person.* By choosing to use the *10 Keys* described in this book, you have chosen to be that adult in your child's life. Feeling, seeing and understanding any person is a basic element in being able to love them. This is especially true for children and teens.

As you seek to understand your child more deeply, your communications—including using the exercises in this book—say to your child that they are loved regardless of their behavior or attitude, and that your love does not depend on what they have done or are doing.

Young people have a "cup" that holds the love they receive from others. This cup of love needs to be filled consistently as it empties on a regular basis.

There are five basic ways to communicate love to a young person. The five specific "love languages" concept describes how to make sure all these basic loving ways are covered in your actions and attitude when connecting and reaching your child.

You can show them love in these 5 different ways:

- **Physical Touch**
- **Words of Affirmation**
- **Quality Time**
- **Gifts**
- **Acts of Service**

Understanding these languages will help in multiple ways, two that are so fundamental they will be mentioned here.

First, understanding the five love languages of people in general will help you in your relationships with all the significant others in your child's life. Helping these relationships be strong will trickle down positively to your child and help build a space of love to support them.

Secondly, the five languages of love will enhance your success as you develop your parenting or teaching skills using the **10 Keys** in this book.

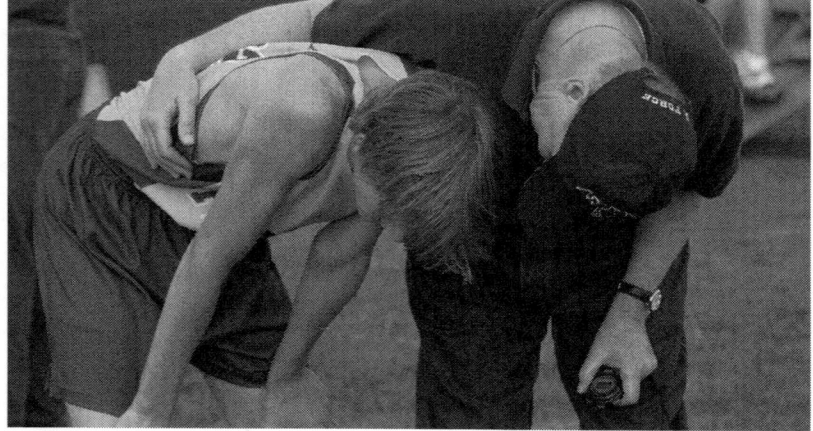

S-1

Based on author Gary Chapman's research, **_each child needs all five of these "languages" to feel loved_**. As they mature into their teens, there is one language that is usually needed more than the others. As they get into their older teen years they settle on one or two preferred languages that may remain as their main "love language" for many years—even throughout their lifetime—with the others having somewhat less importance to them.

As a specific love language emerges as their **_primary,_** you can be tuned into the best way to provide adequate love in the areas that mean the most to your individual child. Mr. Chapman and Mr. Campbell, authors of **_The 5 Love Languages of Children_**, teach there are 5 basic ways to communicate love to your child. In detail, they are:

1. **_Physical Touch_**—Hugs, kisses, tosses and spins, rough play, back and shoulder rubs, high fives, contact sports.

2. **_Words of Affirmation_**—Words of encouragement for a child's efforts, catching them doing something good, and refraining from yelling or angry words that work against affirmation.

3. **_Quality Time_**— Bedtime, car rides, walks, camping, creating memories. Undivided positive attention alone with each child regardless of their current behavior. Good conversation times about current events or telling stories of your personal history.

4. **Gifts**—Genuine and not given as rewards, gifts should serve a purpose for the child and be wrapped or given in a special way, and given just because you care.

5. **Acts of Service**—Something they can't do for themselves, such as when they are ill or over loaded with responsibilities. Helping them with a project, learning a skill or helping them solve a problem. Freely given or done shows them how to serve others and teaches how to make requests and not demands.

As you hone your skill of using these love languages with your child, do not tell them you are doing this or why. If they ask, tell them you are simply

trying to love them in as many ways as you can think of. As in using the other **Keys** in this book just observe and act according to what you think your child needs most at any given time.

Listen to their requests and watch for clues that may give you a hint of what they need or would benefit from

the most. Notice if their requests fall under predominately one love language category.

Continue to be aware if one of the categories of love is their preference to give to others, by noticing if they tend to give you and others hugs and kisses *(#1, Physical Touch)* or take the time to share encouraging words *(#2, Words of Affirmation)*? Do they spend time with an ailing sibling or friend *(#3, Quality Time)*, do they give gifts to show their friendship *(#4, Gifts)*? Do they like to help with tasks around the house and really seem to focus on the importance of the task they are helping with *(#5, Acts of Service)?* We all tend to give to others the love language we want to receive the most and is the easiest one for us to give others.

Mr. Chapman suggests that you can also enhance your understanding by asking your child a preference question of several activities and see which general love language activity they choose. For example, they may want quality time with you right now instead of a gift.

The books that can be used to further your understanding of these concepts are listed in the Bibliography at the end of this book. You can also go to the website *www.5lovelanguages.com* where there are free "tests" for adults and children that can help identify their preferred love languages. Click on the "Profiles" tab on the home page, then on the "Love" link in the drop down menu. There are free specific tests for adults, children and teens. Then click on "Discover your Love

Language" and enjoy taking this fun, easy, and life-enhancing test.

I highly recommend to parents and teachers that they become more familiar with Dr. Chapman's books and concepts, to enhance every area of successful relationships, show love and really "see" your child.

Remember that by combining these 5 love languages consistently when children are young and into their teen years, their "love cup" will continue to be full and you will have a happy, cooperative and content child.

A *different method* must be used when your child becomes a *teenager*. Children enjoy all five languages, but teenagers are markedly on the road to independence. Expressing love in the same ways that were effective when your child was young may cause

your teen to pull away from you as it reminds them of being a "little kid."

While doing all of the 5 languages consistently, you may choose to target one specific language each week to emphasize and note your child's reaction to it. Does one or two stand out as more effective than the others? Keep a log in the "Notes" pages in this book if desired to keep your observations handy.

Another way to discover their current preferred love language is to ask your child or teen the question "I know _____ loves me because they _____." Note what category of language they are describing. Notice how their preferences may change over months or a year, especially when they are quite young.

In Key 1: Review your journal notes for
   Key 1. Notice how the experiences they
   tell you they want to happen or the things
   they want to do fall into categories of the five
   languages of love. Organize your observations
   below. *For example: Wanting to go on vacation
   with my family might indicate that **Quality
   Time** is one of their preferred languages.*

_____

_____

_____

_____

_____

_____

_____

_____

_____

_____

In Key 2: What languages do their favorite experiences most align with? *For example: Expressing themselves through writing and drawing might indicate the importance of **Words of Affirmation, Gifts** or **Acts of Service** depending on why the story was important to them.*

_____

_____

_____

_____

_____

_____

_____

_____

_____

_____

_____

In Key 3: Be aware of the activities and hobbies they showed a passion for. What languages do these relate to? *For example: Music might reflect **Acts of Service** if the music is seen as helping others or **Words of Affirmation** if your child enjoys compliments for their music. Another example is sports, which could suggest **Words of Affirmation** if they like others complimenting them on how well they played.*

_____

_____

_____

_____

_____

_____

_____

_____

_____

_____

_____

_____

S-1

In Key 5: As they shared their dream
future career interests, did any specific
love language surface? *For example: An
interest in a Medical career might show*
Acts of Service. *Or if they show an interest in
being a florist they might relate to* **Gifts** *as they
would enjoy helping others give tokens of love
through a gift of flowers.*

_____

_____

_____

_____

_____

_____

_____

_____

_____

_____

In Key 8: Notice how they like to make a difference for others. There may be clues about their favorite love language, as they are most likely to use the language that speaks love to them in expressing love for others. This is true for adults as well! *For example: Volunteering at the local animal shelter or helping their elderly grandparents may demonstrate a preference for **Acts of Service** as their favorite love language.*

_____

_____

_____

_____

_____

_____

_____

_____

_____

_____

_____

In Key 10: The heroes they look up to and why often demonstrates a love language preference, especially if you ask how they know their hero loves and cares about others. What does that hero do that is important? *For example: If your child loves super-heroes from the comics, this might demonstrate admiration for the **Acts of Service** that the hero performs. If your child looks up to a soccer coach, that could reflect **Words of Affirmation** as the coach praises them for their efforts, or as **Quality Time** for the time the coach spends helping him or her improve their skills.*

_____

_____

_____

_____

_____

_____

_____

_____

_____

Think back to when you were young and how much these languages of love meant when you experienced them. Taking time to show these love languages will magically do for your child what you desired in those days—to feel loved and appreciated. In this loving environment you can plant healthy seeds of belief in their self-value, personal power, goodness and purpose.

One last idea to mention in this short review of this love language topic is about being **contagious**! Like a cold, they can "catch" your love and confidence in them through your communicated belief and your words and actions of love. Here are some **attitudes of belief** you might want to communicate about them:

- A **sense of confidence** that a current situation will turn out well.

- A **sense of achievement** as you help them see progress from where they were just a short time to where they are now.

- A **certainty of positive anticipation** that they will make it through any situation with flying colors. Remind them of the past times when they have succeeded, to ground them in this positive belief for their future.

- A **sense of determination** to use their abilities toward their dreams and visions.

- All of these can be done in ways that reflect the language of love—from the one person who truly believes in their value and purpose of just being who they are—**YOU!**

Journal: My Child's Preferred Love Languages

Now that you have reviewed your journaling and have developed the awareness to identify how the love languages reveal themselves in your child, look for other examples in their day-to-day actions and relationships that reflect the five love languages:

Example 1:_____

_____

_____

   Love language: _____

Example 2:_____

_____

_____

   Love language: _____

Example 3:_____

_____

_____

   Love language: _____

Journal: My Child's Preferred Love Languages (continued)

Example 4:_____

_____

_____

   Love language: _____

Example 5:_____

_____

_____

   Love language: _____

Example 6:_____

_____

_____

   Love language: _____

Example 7:_____

_____

_____

   Love language: _____

Notes:

Notes:

Spare Key 2:
The Importance of Connecting
Your Child with Nature

As parents or teachers, we need to be aware of the importance of helping children of all ages **spend time in nature in an up-close and personal way.** Author Richard Louv's recent book <u>Last Child in the Woods</u> teaches the benefits and concepts of this important **Key** for children's healthy growth and development.

This concept of spending time in nature was taken for granted in former generations, as it was often a necessity of life and time out-of-doors was a normal daily occurrence.

For children (and adults!) being in and interacting with nature brings healing, a sense of peace, a place all their own where they can think, reflect and release the stress of today's fast-paced life. Research clearly shows

time outdoors in free natural unorganized play—in physical contact with nature—brings children joy, inspires creativity, makes space for peace and helps them have a healthy perspective on life. Children benefit biologically, cognitively, spiritually and physically.

Activities such as climbing trees, exploring trails, examining tidal pools, going to the beach, and observing plants and animals is exciting and brings life to all the child's senses, while triggering curiosity and wonder.

Just intellectually "knowing" about the plants and animals in their world through computers or television is not the same as physically "experiencing" nature for themselves. Starting at a very young age, children need to have intimate positive contact with nature for their healthy growth, problem-solving skill development, a quickening of their thinking processes and building a healthy relationship with the earth. Learning to pay attention to how the natural world works is a critical

component of life and part of learning the decision-making process.

Being in nature is different than organized sports, which is based on following directions in a very structured and controlled way. Free interaction with nature provides a sense of freedom for children especially in our more crowded cities and increased regulations in our communities due to safety and liability concerns, and is essential for these young people to grow into healthy, balanced mature adults. The benefits are huge and with parents, teachers or other responsible adults within eyesight, it is safe and incredibly important and rewarding for both child and adult.

Research shows the potential for harm due to accidents or "strangers" is far less than many people believe. It has now been proven that *not* going out into nature is more damaging for children.

Let me share a clear example I experienced a few days ago as I took Mr. Louv's book and my paper to the beach for a day of reading and writing.

Example of the Benefits of Children Being in Nature: A Recent Observation

One day a short time ago as I sat at the beach with my books and chapters to edit I was surrounded by two families with small children.

As I read and worked, it was heartwarming to watch the two sets of parents sharing this wonderful

end of summer beach experience with their children. On my left was a mom and dad with a young girl named Libby (her real name as I overheard as her parents were chatting so close by).

As they put up their shade tent and spread out all the sand toys this little dark haired girl about four years old set to digging with her toy shovel. A few minutes later as the parents tried to coax her to the quiet waters edge she showed fear. With the persistence of her mom she finally went to the water's edge, but was afraid to let it touch her feet. Upon its touch she ran back toward the tent to what she assumed was a safe distance from the sea.

As I sat under my umbrella nearby with the book titled _Last Child in the Woods,_ Libby approached me. I guess I looked like the safe grandmotherly type who could protect and persuade her parents that this water idea was not in her best interest.

As she approached, with her mom not too far behind, she said to me, "I don't want to go by the water."

By this time she was almost upon me with her mom right behind, possibly fearing this stranger might not appreciate this interruption by her little one.

I was amused by this whole series of events. I reached out and said to her, "Give this book to your mom to see, it is a very important book for her to know about."

Libby took the book I handed to her (_Last Child in the Woods_) and as she held it for a moment she saw the picture on the front of the little boy

holding the frog. Libby handed the book to her mom and at the same time asked me "What is the book about?" She seemed a very intelligent child and curious.

I quietly and calmly in a respectful tone said it is a book about the importance of children like her going to see things like the water and all the shells that were there for her to discover and put in her bucket. There might be little fish for her to find and the water was here to play with her.

By this time her mom had arrived and was looking at the book.

Libby was thoughtful for a moment, then she asked me what the little boy's name was whose picture was on the front of the book. My quick thinking mind gave him the name "Kevin" and I went on the describe how good it is for people, especially little people, to go and be around the water, animals and plants with their parents.

Her mom commented how much she liked the book and was interested in purchasing one for her own reading and enhanced parenting.

Her grateful look for my supportive comments was clear as now a receptive Libby went happily to the water–and I was rewarded with several hours of reading and observing as she and her parents discovered many beautiful shells, sea creatures and the many wonders of playing in the sea. It was interesting for me see her developing her thinking and problem-solving skills as the small waves impacted the little castle she was building and decorating. She had so much fun spending loving quality time in dad's arms wading out into the water.

To my right was a young family with two boys about the age of three and six.

The Gulf Of Mexico that day was unusually calm, flat and crystal clear.

These boys showed no fear of the environment and rejoiced instantly at being near the water's edge.

Their dad had brought a paddle board that obviously was a cherished item for him.

In a few minutes dad asked the boys if they wanted to go exploring on the water with him on the paddle board. Mom gladly agreed as she could have some alone time on the blanket relaxing feeling the rays of the sun as she laid out to rest.

With life preservers on, the three adventurers headed out over the crystal blue waters.

But soon you could hear the littlest one crying out for mama. Quickly they were back with the little boy climbing off and sprinting for the blanket to be in the safe proximity of mom.

Again the explorers set out with only two brave souls on board.

They went far out where there were about a dozen paddle boarders exploring where the water was a little deeper and a rich shade of dark blue.

About thirty minutes later dad and this older boy came back telling of the amazing sights they had seen. Schools of fish described by their arms stretched out wide being followed by even bigger fish swimming right

under their boards. They saw sea turtles and dolphins playing. It was wonderful as I listened to the stories of the fun they had on their adventure.

Over the next few hours this family of four spent quality time and explored the fun of the shallow waters, trying to catch small fish with their nets and building castles in the sand.

They ate lunch together and the littlest one took a short nap on mom's shoulder, while another trip by the two brave explorers reaped more amazing tales of adventure and wonders they beheld from the safety of the paddle board.

Now awake, the littlest one wanted to try joining in the adventures again, instructed by dad that this time he could come if he didn't cry out for mom on the journey.

Upon negotiating this requirement the littlest one agreed, donned his life jacket and set out making this again the expedition of three.

Strong, brave, dad standing tall and paddling smoothly took his boys to find yet another adventure. This time as the littlest one joined them, his fear was replaced with curiosity for the journey.

Again thirty minutes later they all safely returned with great enthusiasm for the big fish they saw and how they could see the bottom about twenty feet below.

Each had stories to tell of the wonderful experience they had and raced up the sand to find mom resting on the blanket. The littlest child was happy in his bravery of going out with the others.

He learned he was safe without taking mom along, and that the world of nature held many wonders he might never see if he stayed on the blanket. As the sun began to go past high noon the three children discovered each other. They played happily together racing up and down the ledge of sand that was left by the former weekend storm's powerful waves, they built sand castles together and had a great time. The oldest boy learned the importance of his role of being the leader and responsible for not taking the others so far away to the big dunes from a brief conversation with his dad.

The day was rewarding for all involved. The parents spent quality time building character in their children, making lifetime memories, and enjoying a time of shared *love. The children learned how fun it is to be in a natural setting, freely using their thinking skills and the joy of adventure. I cherished a perfect natural example of the principals of the powerful book of helping children spend quality time in nature with all its benefits.*

This example is exactly why I am dedicating several pages in this book to share this important concept with you wonderful parents and teachers, who are taking the time to expand your skills and wisdom in helping your children.

Encouragement of free and natural outdoor play is an essential element for our children to grow into healthy, caring individuals as it teaches respect for all aspects of life and helps build acceptance for diversity on the earth. Nature gives itself to children and shows them how to use their power, teaches about challenges while enlarging their capacity for wonder. It brings a sense of calm, focus and excitement while teaching them to use all their senses—something that time with electronic devices does not do. Playing, walking, riding bikes, gardening, visiting nature reserves, parks, zoos, botanical gardens, nature trails and camping trips are some great examples of nature experiences. It might be as easy as exploring in the back yard, at the end of the street or in the vacant lot next door.

In contrast, research is beginning to reveal that children and young people being constantly involved in organized play such as sports may actually ***inhibit*** the development of the creative thinking needed for life success. In the past, parents could count on their

children going on school field trips and having some natural play time at school. The trend of focusing on test-centric education here in the U.S., along with fears of liability, may have reduced student time for recess or organized physical education. These factors may be part of why we see rising obesity and reduced mental acuity and concentration in children. Time spent experiencing nature seems to enhance these skills, while reducing stress and anxiety. Plus, children need unstructured ways to play in nature to simply get their energy out in a healthy way!

Too much time indoors creating a sedentary lifestyle has been linked to mental health and obesity issues in children. Being indoors excessively may diminish their use of the senses, may add to attention difficulties, higher rates of physical and emotional illness and depression.

I highly recommend reading Mr. Louv's book, and following the ideas that fit your family to bring this important component to the personal growth of your child.

Including natural out-of-doors time in your weekly schedule may bring great benefits for everyone in your family, by reducing stress for both you and your child, while increasing health and creating life-long memories. The restorative environment of nature can provide a place where the child's mind can really relax and simply take in the natural environment. The result? A sense of peace, clearer thinking and focus. Ah…taking time to breathe the fresh air…relax…This is good for you dad, mom, teacher and children!

Its easy…nature is everywhere…just walk outside!

Conclusion:
A Cry of Their Heart: "Please *See* and *Hear* Me Deeply"

Congratulations for being such a caring person for your child by using this book. Even if you did only part of the **Keys**, you have made a beautiful and profound difference in their lives forever!

The little natural conversations suggested in this book are practical ways to hear your child's heart. Paying attention to your children and young adults in these ways allows you to guide them along the pathways that fit them. "Seeing" and "Hearing" your child deeply over time—regardless of their occasional acting-out behavior—is healing and brings strength to children.

Taking time to do this will make your parenting or teaching role so much easier, and can be key to keeping you close to your young people through your time with them, with far-reaching implications throughout their lives.

A Personal Note to Parents and Teachers:

Thank you for joining me on this journey to wholeness in your child—no matter where or in what country you live, whether at home or in the classroom.

They are part of the balance of life and learning to be who they are is critical for the world to be a good place for everyone.

From now on, continually being a detective looking for clues about your child can be a fun and interesting experience for you. You will discover there is a *"map" hidden in their hearts* that will help guide you and them along a path that supports their healthy growth into adulthood. Watch for clues that the map will give you both along the way by listening to their answers to your questions.

Help your child choose wisely the kinds of *friendships* that will support and nurture them along their path to success. As they enjoy learning to be who they are, selecting friends will be easier and more in alignment with what nurtures them.

Relax and know *you can't make a mistake* and you can't get this wrong. There may be some bumps along the way, but if you persevere, your children will repay you a hundredfold by becoming healthy well-adjusted individuals.

The goal is for each child to find their unique calling on the earth by living their purpose, which is simply **to be who they are**, and celebrating the unique gift they are to themselves and the world.

In summary, the emphasis of this book, **_10 Easy Keys To Unlocking Kids' Passion and Purpose_** is about training and building the awareness and skills of parents and teachers by taking the time to simply notice and bring into focus a child's natural talents and passions.

Asking, observing and journaling are essential for these goals to be reached. Enjoy the journey as you help unlock **YOUR** child's passion and purpose!

Remember to Celebrate with Your Child

Celebration is the key to keeping the cycle of productivity moving along for us all. Teach your young people to notice and celebrate the special qualities about themselves and the little and big things they accomplish. Celebrate that being who they are makes a profound difference in their life and the world.

Each person is unique and needs to see clearly who and how they benefit the world by just their presence and living the life that fits them. Like a piece of a giant  puzzle we each have a very important part to play in making the world a place of happiness and peace for all that share our wonderful planet.

Animals seem to know just where and how they fit into the balance of life. Now it is time for all of us to follow their example and excel with our individual, wonderful talents to expand our world into the next level of all it can be!

Be blessed as you begin the most important opportunity of your life–discovering the wonderful children that fill your life with wonder and joy.

The 10 Easy Keys:

KEY 1: Discovering Your Child's Dream Life List

KEY 2: Exploring Life Purpose Awareness–
The Key to Success

KEY 3: Using Spare Time — A Valuable Asset
for Learning Life Skills

KEY 4: Celebrating Natural and Learned Skills

KEY 5: Seeing Into Your Child's Future Career Path

KEY 6: Seeing the Life/School/Career Connetion

KEY 7: Developing the Habits of Tenacity and
Perseverance

KEY 8: Noticing How Your Child Makes a Difference

KEY 9: Building Communication Skills —
Genuine Listening

KEY 10: Using The Hero Connection

Plus...

SPARE KEY 1: Your Child's "Love Languages"

SPARE KEY 2: The Importance of Connecting
Your Child with Nature

Bibliography

Chapman, Gary and Campbell, Ross
  The 5 Love Languages of Children,
  Chicago, Illinois. Northfield Publishing, 2012

Chapman, Gary *The 5 Love Languages of Teenagers*,
  Chicago, Illinois. Northfield Publishing, 2010

Covey, Stephen R. *The Seven Habits of Highly Effective
  People*, Provo, Utah. Covey Leadership Center,
  1990

Covey, Sean. *The Seven Habits of Highly Effective
  Teens*, New York, New York. Fireside/Simon &
  Schuster, Inc., 1998

Louv, Richard, *Last Child In The Woods,* Chapel Hill,
  North Carolina. Algonquin Books of Chapel Hill,
  2008

Appendix

This section contains support materials to use with the *10 Easy Keys* and *2 Spare Keys* to enhance your experience and success.

"Feeling" Words

The words listed below can be helpful when encouraging your child to express feelings. This is especially helpful in the exercises in *Key 2*.

Happy words:

pleased

glad

wonderful

elated

excited

content

surprised

proud

relieved

satisfied

confident

healthy

intrigued

cleansed

connected

loved

joyful

Positive words:

calm

clear

secure

challenged

strong

adequate

rejuvenated

safe

free

trustworthy

trusting

liked

smart

worthwhile

cared for

important

belong

determined

forgiving

hopeful

motivated

inspired

daring

energetic

loving

eager

excited

receptive

happy

hyped

adventurous

My Perfect Day—Examples from 9th Grade Students

"My perfect day would have three of my favorite things in it. The first thing would be waking up to the sound of the ocean and the peaceful wind. The next things would have to be tubing all day on the sparkling water. The third thing would be letting the waves crashing into each other put me to sleep on the shore.

"So the first part of my perfect day would be waking up to the sounds of the ocean and wind. I love the beach when it's a nice windy day. Some consider it too hot and sweaty. But I consider the beach as an amazing way to relax and have a good time.

"The next event that would have to take place would be tubing. Tubing to me is the most fun anyone can ever have. I got more adrenaline built up tubing then I do during a football game. I remember the last time I went tubing. That afterwards I had a huge crash because of all the adrenaline I had went through that

day. So I just think the tubing is just a great way to spend time with family and friends.

"The last thing that would have to happen would be falling asleep in the cool sound. With the waves crashing into each other." — Koleman

"The perfect day would be waking up to a nice crisp fall morning and a big plate of scrambled eggs and sausage for breakfast. Next I would get all dressed in my warm clothes, and my dad and I would head to the woods for a hike. We would see lots of interesting wildlife and take photos of the colored leaves." – Dustin

"My perfect day would be waking up in the a.m. and my dad tells me 'You are going to England to meet One Direction!' So I eat a good breakfast and hop in the shower and get dressed to head off to the airport to board the plane to England.

"When the plane lands my heart feels like it's gonna explode I'm so nervous cause I don't know what to say and I don't know what to expect, all these emotions are zooming through my head.

"When I get my luggage there are five boys standing with a sign that says my name. I walk over and tell them 'that's me!' So we get into the limo and drive to a big house. When I get there they say, 'I'm Liam, Harry, Hall, Zany, Louis' nice to meet you. All along I had nothing to worry about because they were very nice."
– Makayla

*"My perfect day started when I woke up in Destin!
'Wow, how did we end up in a beach house!' I said.
Then my parents walked into my room and said, 'Austin,
this is your special day! You can do anything you want!'
Then dad added, 'I thought to myself about parasailing!
I remember how you would love parasailing. Is there
anything else?'*

*"So we went to the beach to go parasailing. I was
a little scared at fist, but I was so happy that I got to go.
It was amazing, the speed boat is at high speeds. I was
going so high I saw a wonderful view of Destin. Then
I was getting lowered into the water and half of my body
was submerged!"*   *– Austin*

Other students mentioned things like water parks,
shopping with friends and unlimited funds, laughter,
returning to a home city, slumber parties, eating out or
cooking in, going to the mall, dressing up and going out
with friends, watching movies, four wheelers or go carts
with family, watching or participating in sports events,
doing a mechanical project with their dads, hunting
and camping, building things on the computer, travel
overseas, waking up without an alarm clock and restful
relaxation. From telling these stories, students were
able to get a clearer picture of the general areas that are
important to their happiest experiences.

Authors Note: I was amazed by how few
mentioned playing video games and technology. They
almost always described outdoor activities, as well as
the most delicious breakfasts and other meals with
many details of the food and the way it smelled, looked
and tasted.

Activities/Hobbies:
What gets YOUR CHILD excited?

Below you'll find a list of many activities and hobbies that youth enjoy in their spare time, and that can lead to satisfying careers as your child applies important skills. Check off all that interest your child, or about which they would like to find out more! Then, rank #1, #2, and #3 of your child's MOST favorite activities. Write these in your journal.

____ Acting
____ Archery
____ Art classes
____ Astronomy
____ Birdwatching/birding
____ Blogging
____ BMXing
____ Board games and tabletop games
____ Bodybuilding
____ Boxing
____ Calligraphy
____ Camping
____ Computer programming or game developing
____ Collecting interesting, bizarre, unique items (stamps, candy containers, buttons, bottle lids, ticket stubs, old postcards, etc.)
____ Create a webcomic and get some followers
____ Cycling
____ Dancing (ballroom, hip hop, ballet, etc.)
____ Debating (start or join a club at school or community center)

____ Dioramas
____ Doodling (and upload your drawings onto a Tumblr!)
____ Drawing
____ Film (anime, kung fu, sci fi, documentary, etc.)
____ Finance and investing
____ Form a band, or grab some friends and just jam
____ Freestyle rapping
____ Gardening
____ Genealogy
____ Geocaching (hunting objects using compasses)
____ Hiking
____ Hobby electronics or hobby engineering
____ Horse riding
____ Hunting
____ Learn a foreign language
____ Make greeting cards
____ Martial arts
____ Mechanics
____ Metal working
____ Meteorology
____ Martial arts (karate, tae kwon doe, etc.)
____ Model railroads and miniature trains

_____ Mountain biking
_____ Musical Instruments and music making
_____ Nature conservation hobbies and projects
_____ Newspaper or newsletter writing (for your school, club or local community of artists or gamers, etc.)
_____ Oil Painting
_____ Origami (paper folding)
_____ Penpal writing (postcards or letters or send fun, handmade items)
_____ Photography
_____ Play guitar, piano, drums, trombone, trumpet, or sing
_____ Poker
_____ Pottery (take a class with a parent or friend)
_____ Publish a Zine
_____ Radio Controlled electronics projects (cars, boats, aircraft, etc.)
_____ Radios (ham radio or try making your own podcast/ internet radio station)
_____ Reading (fiction, non-fiction, poetry, short stories, autobio, memoir, etc.)
_____ Robotics (make a simple robot)
_____ Rock climbing
_____ Running (you could train for a marathon event)
_____ Scrapbooks
_____ Sewing or fashion design

_____ Skateboarding
_____ Skiing, snowboarding (and other winter sports)
_____ Social media technology
_____ Solar power electronic projects (make a solar USB charger, etc.)
_____ Sports, team (soccer, basketball, football, baseball, softball, etc.)
_____ Street art and circus hobbies
_____ Swimming (lifeguard training, for example)
_____ Sword fighting or fencing
_____ Tennis
_____ Volunteering
_____ Watercolor painting
_____ Water sports: surfing, rafting, sailing, power boating, scuba diving
_____ Weightlifting
_____ Wood working
_____ Wrestling and other combat sports
_____ Writing (journalism, poetry, fiction, short stories, essays, etc.)
_____ Yoga
_____ Other:_____
_____ Other:_____
_____ Other:_____
_____ Other:_____
_____ Other:_____
_____ Other:_____

Example Weekly Planning Chart *Dates: from* _____ *to* _____

	SUNDAY	MONDAY	TUESDAY
5 am-6 am			
6 am-7 am		Dress, get ready for school	→
7 am-8 am		School	→
8 am-9 am			
9 am-10 am			
10 am-11 am	Family time		
11 am-12 noon			
12 noon-1 pm			
1 pm-2 pm			
2 pm-3 pm	Activity: music		
3 pm-4 pm			
4 pm-5 pm		Homework	Soccer
5 pm-6 pm		Home chores	
6 pm-7 pm	Dinner	Dinner	
7 pm-8 pm	Homework	Activity: music	Dinner
8 pm-9 pm			Homework
9 pm-10 pm	Get ready for school (backpack, clothes, homework check.....) In bed by 10... TV, phones and computers off... SLEEP!		

128 **10 Easy Keys To Unlocking Kids' Passion & Purpose**

Note: This example of a student's weekly planning included school time and homework, but also shows how spare time was used for the student's activities (in this case, music), family time, home chores, etc.)

WEDNESDAY	THURSDAY	FRIDAY	SATURDAY
			Unscheduled time is important! This is when young people can spend **unstructured** time out in nature, reading for pleasure, having social interactions, etc. Overscheduling kids creates stress, and keeps them from learning how to use their free time wisely!
			Home chores
			Activity: hiking
Music lesson	*Homework*		
Homework	*Home chores*	*Dinner*	
Dinner	*Dinner*		*Dinner*
Activity: music		*Go to game*	

Thank You Note Writing Instructions

Did someone give you an opportunity to learn more about their job?

Did a person take time to share about the path they followed to the career they love?

If so, why not take a few minutes to let that person know how much their actions meant to you by writing a handwritten thank you note?

This only takes a few minutes and will mean so much to that person.

Thank You

Writing a thank you note after a job shadow visit is very important.

This note builds a connection between you and this person which can last a long time and may be an important networking tool for a later time when you are looking for a meaningful career either before or after graduation.

Writing these notes are best done **within three days** after your job shadow experience and are written personally to the person with whom you visited.

Keep a list of who you visited with, when this visit happened and the date you wrote the thank you note for future reference.

Here are some simple steps to writing a short meaningful thank you note.

• *Choose your paper:*

There are many types of thank you cards in the stores from classy types of professional cards with embossed words with thank you in gold or silver ink right down to the cute ones with flowers or animals. For professional communication either the more formal classy or a nice sheet of stationary might be the best type to use. However, the type of card or stationary is not as important as the content. It's really up to you.

• *The Three Paragraph Format:*

Relax with the knowledge you don't have to be like a famous author or poet. Just simply expressing sincerely from your heart is all it takes to share your appreciation. And it means so much to the recipient.

The three paragraphs could look like this:

1. Paragraph One is a few simple words such as "Thank you for taking time to visit with me on _____ (date) about your career"

2. Write a few sentences about your experience. Include some little detail of how the visit was interesting or helpful to you.

3. Finalize your message with one last thank you by closing with a sentence or two.

It's as simple as that! On the next page are some examples to get you started!

Thank You Note Examples

Example 1:

Dear Mr. Lee,

Thank you so much for meeting with me last Tuesday, September 10.

I appreciated learning about how much you enjoy your career as a senior mechanic at the auto dealership. It was helpful for me to realize how you got your education and training to prepare you specifically for working on this type of car and to have a career in this speciality area.

The extra part about your military experience was helpful as I am thinking of exploring that career option also in the near future.

Thank you again for taking time to share your experience and how you enjoy what you do at work everyday.

Sincerely,
David

Example 2:

Dear Mrs. Harris,

It was so nice of you to take time to meet with me last Tuesday, October 1st to share information about your music and entertainment career.

The music you sang and played was awesome—thanks for sharing your CD's with me, and telling me about how you made your recordings. I also liked the way you talked about pushing through the tough times to accomplish the dreams you had in your heart.

It will inspire me to keep following my goals in the entertainment industry that I see for myself, allowing the twists and turns to happen and never give up.

I hope some day to be able to share with you of my success and help inspire others as you have inspired me.

Thank you again for the valuable experience and for your example.

Sincerely,
Breland

YOUR KEY, YOUR DOOR
Teaching Guides:

CLASSROOM TEACHER'S NOTES
**For Large Group and
Classroom Youth Teaching**

This comprehensive 110-page
teacher's guide is *specifically*
designed for use in classrooms and
with large groups. An 8-1/2" x 11"
teacher's companion to the *YKYD*
book, loaded with practical tools to
use in guiding their students in this
unique process. This step-by-step guide includes **Pre-Work,
Class Discussion** and **Teaching Techniques** sections for
each chapter in the *YKYD* book, plus lesson plan examples,
over 20 copy-ready handouts, and 15 additional career and
business success concepts.

978-0-9856235-2-4

Available at *www.doorknobbooks.com*

INSTRUCTOR'S GUIDE
For Parents and Small Groups

This helpful 55-page guide is
designed *specifically* to be used
by parents, instructors of groups
of up to eight youth, and in home-
school settings. With specific,
step-by-step guidance about
*What You Need, How To Prepare,
Activity Instruction*, and *"On
The Wall"* display ideas, this guide enables parents and
instructors of small groups to successfully facilitate the
child's exciting journey of self-discovery using the *YKYD*
book. This book is available as a free download on
www.doorknobbooks.com.

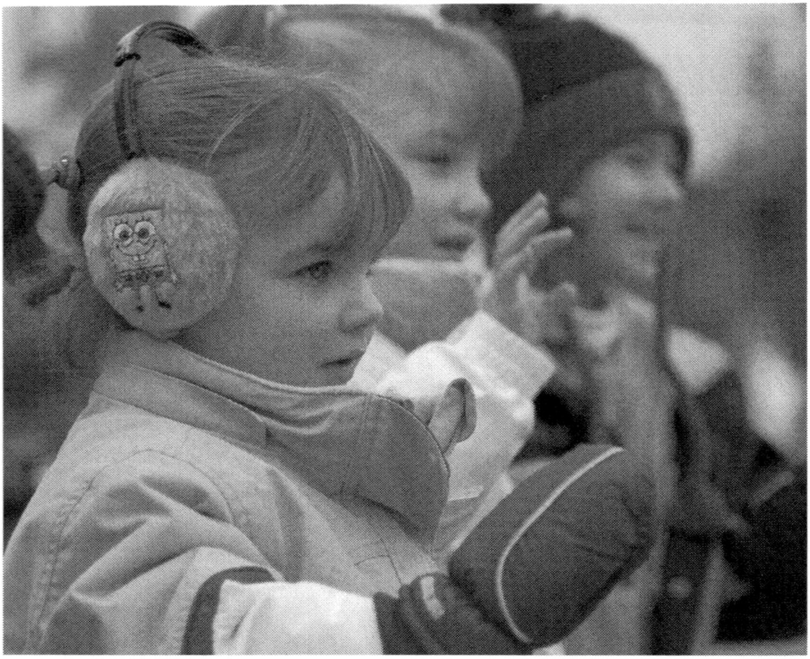

Notes: